Behaviour 4 My Future

An emotional literacy programme for students at risk of exclusion

Susie Davis

Please check front pocket for CD

A Speechmark Behaviour Management Resource

Behaviour 4 My Future

An emotional literacy programme for students at risk of exclusion

Susie Davis

Published by
Speechmark Publishing Ltd, 70 Alston Drive, Bradwell Abbey,
Milton Keynes MK13 9HG, UK
Tel: +44 (0) 1908 326 944   Fax: +44 (0) 1908 326 960
www.speechmark.net

First published 2008

002-5458/Printed in the United Kingdom/1010

British Library Cataloguing in Publication Data
Davis, Susie
  Behaviour 4 My Future
  1. Behaviour modification – Great Britain 2. Classroom
  management – Great Britain 3. School children – Great
  Britain – Attitudes
  I. Title
  371.5

ISBN 978 0 86388 682 9

Contents

Acknowledgements . . . . **vii**

Introduction . . . . **viii**

Student Behaviour viii

What Is Emotional Literacy? ix

Setting Up and Delivering *Behaviour 4 My Future* **1**

Getting Students and Parents on Board 1

Staff Awareness 1

Session Times 1

Weekly Self-review 1

Group Rules 1

Delivery of the Programme 2

Using Behaviour Data 2

Meeting the Students 3

The Behaviour Charter **4**

Session 1: Reputations, Exclusion, Behaviour and Me! **5**

Baseline – Lesson Audit 7

Reputations, Exclusion, Behaviour and Me! 8

Agree 10

Disagree 11

Not sure 12

The Key Question Is... 13

Answer... 14

Session 2: My Future ... What Does It Hold? **15**

My Future ... What Does It Hold? 17

My Here and Now 19

Session 3: Thinking, Feeling and Behaviour **23**

Search for the Feeling Words! 25

My Feelings About My School 26

Thinking, Feeling and Behaviour – Jack's Story 28

Session 4: What Affects How I Feel About School? **29**

What Affects How I Feel About School? 31

Face the Problem and Solve It! – Example 32

Face the Problem and Solve It! 33

Session 5: What's Motivation all About? **35**

What's Motivation All About? 37

So ... What's It Going to Take to Motivate You to Avoid Exclusion
and Have a Better Future? 38

Session 6: What Can Affect My Motivation? **39**

What Can Affect My Motivation? 41

Get Your Head in the Right Place 42

Session 7: Goal Setting **43**

Goal Setting 45
My Goal for this School Year 46
Top Tips for Achieving Your Goal 47

Session 8: Getting a Grip on My Anger **49**

Getting a Grip on My Anger 52
Managing My Anger Self-assessment 53
What is Anger Anyway? 54
The Anger Perception Game – Statements 55
People Who Fly into a Rage 56

Session 9: Triggers and Chillers! **57**

What Makes You Angry? 59
Take Control and Chill Out! 60
The Management Recipe! 61

Session 10: Stressed Out! **63**

Feeling Stressed 65
Emotional Symptoms of Stress 66
Physical Symptoms of Stress 67
Strategies for Managing that Stress 68
Top Tips for Coping with that Stress 69

Session 11: Surviving the Classroom **71**

Surviving the Classroom 72
Surviving the Classroom – Response Cards 74

Session 12: Multiple Intelligences – What's It All About? .. **75**

Multiple Intelligences – What's It All About? 77
Famous People – What Kind of Intelligences Do They Have? 78
My Multiple Intelligence Profile 79

Session 13: Review, Reflection and Progress **83**

Success is More About Having the Right Attitude 85
Word Conundrum 86
Word Conundrum – Facilitator's Answer Sheet 88
Progress – Lesson Audit 90
Certificate of Achievement 91

School of Emotional Literacy **92**

Acknowledgements

My thanks must go to all the students I have worked with along the way over the last 17 years, whose experiences, feelings and openness have given me many ideas and the motivation to write another emotional literacy programme.

Many thanks must also go to Rachel Carter who would not let me forget that I said I would write this resource! Thank you, Rachel, for your gentle persuasion to get on with it, which I really needed – you are a real gem!

I would also like to thank a great team of people who have made my first experience of working for a school rather than the Local Authority such an enjoyable one. So, thank you to Steve Moir, Matt Smith, Maxine Houghton and Debbie Pearce – it's a pleasure working with you all.

Finally – to my own family, Shannon, Sheamus and Jack, who are very tolerant when I go into laptop drive and just let me get on with it.

Susie Davis

Introduction

Student Behaviour

As far as classroom behaviour is concerned staff are the most important people in the classroom. It is their behaviour that is the principal factor in avoiding students' disruption. A teacher's behaviour and attitude will influence and affect how students behave. The evidence for this is obvious. Classes and students behave differently for different teachers.

(Middlesbrough LEA, 2003)

This quotation highlights an important point. Indeed, I have never worked with a student who behaved in exactly the same way for every subject teacher! Student behaviour is influenced by so many factors, of which the quality of a student's relationship with the teacher is a significant one: the better the relationship, the more positive the behaviour.

Understanding this is in itself a revelation for many students: thinking then about why it is that they don't get on well with some teachers is the next, while doing something about it is the biggest hurdle. Relationships are a two-way process. We cannot expect students to build them on their own: as adults we have a responsibility to form positive relationships with the students in our care – this is vital for learning.

In April 2007, the then Department for Education and Skills (now the Department for Children, Schools and Families) launched the Secondary Social and Emotional Aspects to Learning (SEAL), a long-awaited resource following on from the Primary SEAL which has been instrumental in enhancing the emotional literacy skills of thousands of students. Improved levels of emotional literacy are known to improve self-esteem, learning, behaviour and attendance; thus its importance in terms of being implemented at secondary level is clear.

However, there is more to improving emotional literacy than simply teaching students a set of personal and social competencies. To truly make a difference, schools need to lead from the top and put in place a policy that implements emotional literacy at every level, from the caretaker to the staff room, from the kitchen staff to the senior leadership of the school. Everyone in the school community needs to model, demonstrate, teach and value the principles of emotional literacy, and seek to create a community that supports its development in every area of the curriculum and school experience. It would be a mistake simply to limit SEAL to one subject area, such as PSHE. Developing an ethos of inclusion goes hand in hand with the need to develop emotional literacy, in order to create an environment which enhances the emotional health and well-being of everyone in the school community.

As with the Primary SEAL resource, there will be students whose experiences, attitudes and behaviour require a more person-centred approach, and it is this that has motivated the writing of this resource. For many students across the secondary phase, their social, emotional and behavioural needs impede their learning, alienate them from their school community and leave them with low levels of self-esteem and a poor self-image.

Early intervention is crucial for these students, and this resource has been written to support students whose behaviour places them at risk of exclusion from school. It seeks to motivate, inspire and enable students to make better choices, as well as to develop skills and attitudes that allow them to enjoy and achieve. They will develop a more motivated and optimistic outlook concerning who they are and what really matters, which in turn will lead them to take control over their destiny rather than simply being disaffected 'passengers'.

What Is Emotional Literacy?

Emotional literacy is a set of personal and social competencies which, when developed, enhance areas of our lives. It includes:

- ☐ Self-awareness: a personal competency – understanding ourselves, the journey we have been on and how people and events in our lives have affected the way we think and feel about ourselves; recognising how we think and feel and how this can affect our behaviour if we allow it to.

- ☐ Managing feelings: a personal competency – moving on from our ability to label and talk about our feelings, this domain requires us to be able to manage our emotions effectively, not only the often destructive emotion of anger but also the optimistic states; balancing our thoughts and feelings with the needs of others when we react.

- ☐ Motivation: a personal competency – if we don't feel motivated, how are we going to achieve our goals? This is a key attitude to encourage and one which, when students have it, takes them on to a new level.

- ☐ Empathy: a social competency – understanding other people's needs and feelings, showing people that we can react appropriately when they are angry, upset, sad, and so on; recognising emotions in others and taking them into account.

- ☐ Social skills: a social competency – getting along with others is crucial. Our ability to communicate effectively, listen to others, take turns, and so forth, means that we have sound social skills.

I hope that students and teachers alike will find the sessions in this course both worthwhile and enjoyable.

Setting Up and Delivering
Behaviour 4 My Future

This programme is designed to be delivered by any professional working with students whose behaviour places them at risk of exclusion from school.

It is easy to use and each session includes a brief introduction, a list of the secondary SEAL outcomes associated with it, and a step-by-step guide to delivery. The worksheets for each session follow these, in the order in which they are designed to be delivered.

Getting Students and Parents on Board

Students whose behaviour places them at risk of exclusion often have difficult relationships in school with some of their teachers and other students. It is therefore of paramount importance, before starting group work or one-to-one support, that you spend time getting to know each student. This time is a great investment in beginning to establish a positive relationship: students are more open to learning if they like and feel they have built a rapport with the person who is teaching them.

Likewise, the connection with home cannot be overestimated. It is also worth taking the time to write to all the parents of students you have identified for the course. Alternatively, a phone call home is an opportunity to gain an insight into parental perceptions of a student's behaviour and to make that crucial link between the student's home life and the school.

Staff Awareness

Relationships are so vital if you are to succeed in supporting students in improving their behaviour. Encouraging the students' teachers to use appropriate and meaningful praise with the students, to acknowledge their participation and encourage their progress, really does make a difference. Students do appreciate it if someone notices their positive behaviours, not simply their negative ones.

Session Times

Each session is designed to last for one normal school period. If you haven't managed to finish all the suggested work in a session, simply carry it forward to the next week. Try to spend as much time as possible encouraging students to talk about and share their experiences with each other: for these students this is as important as the suggested work.

Weekly Self-review

Encourage students to reflect on their progress each week and allow the entire group to give feedback. If students have had a difficult week, allow time for them to be listened to, and support them in finding their own solutions.

Group Rules

As with any group work, it is advisable to establish a set of group rules before beginning the course. Involve students in agreeing these rules to ensure they have ownership of them.

Delivery of the Programme

Drawing on the wealth of information available to us regarding the way in which our brains learn, I would suggest that the following points are considered before delivering the programme:

- ☐ Opportunities should be provided regularly for students to stop and discuss what they have learned. Encourage them to think about how this new information might affect them.

- ☐ Make sure that your group is fully attentive and ready to begin the first session before you start delivering the programme. Use fun energisers and brain gym activities if you feel that attention levels are dropping.

- ☐ Make your delivery upbeat and lively!

- ☐ Think about using background music. Brain research shows us that music can be used as a mood enhancer, increasing the release of emotions, positively affecting physical energy, and stimulating creativity and thinking power.

- ☐ Consider inviting other people along to add interest and different teaching styles to the sessions; this will also add diversity.

- ☐ Water is so important: don't have dehydrated learners in the room with you! Provide drinking water during the sessions.

- ☐ Think about the learning environment: heat, lighting, space, ventilation and colour.

- ☐ Be prepared to deliver the sessions in ways that will support different learning styles.

- ☐ You need to engage positive emotions; this will make it easier for these students to learn. Be positive with them and create a warm, safe and welcoming environment.

Using Behaviour Data

Most schools now hold behaviour data on their system. This data is easily accessible and should be a starting point for any intervention. From this data you will be able to identify a cohort of students whose poor behaviour is preventing them from learning and achieving. Look for patterns within this data:

- ☐ **Times of day when incidents are more prevalent**: too much sugary food at break time; diet issues?

- ☐ **Particular teachers**: difficult relationships?

- ☐ **Subject area**: difficulty in accessing the curriculum; teaching and learning styles?

- ☐ **Day of the week**: students returning to school following a difficult weekend, for example?

This data will act as your baseline for the course and allow you to discuss areas of concern directly with the student or particular teacher. If necessary, and to give the students a fresh start, a restorative approach could be used in circumstances where a student has disrupted a lesson for so long that their reputation may get in the way of progress. This would need to be done with the prior agreement of all parties and with a clear aim to seek a positive way forward.

Meeting the Students
Session 1 could be an opportunity for you to meet with the students on a one-to-one basis and to complete their behaviour and lesson audit. As mentioned earlier, you need to get the students on board: completing the audit on a one-to-one basis may allow some more personal exploration.

Students might be given a folder in which to collect their work from the sessions that make up the course.

The Behaviour Charter

☐ I am responsible for my own behaviour at all times.

☐ I always have a choice as to how I decide to behave.

☐ If I believe I can make good choices, I will get there in the end.

☐ I believe in myself and feel motivated to improve.

☐ If I don't get it right the first, second or third time, I will keep trying.

☐ When I am faced with a challenge, I will not give up.

☐ I believe that everyone has the right to be treated with respect – there is no excuse for behaviour that hurts others (teachers and students).

☐ I believe that everyone has the right to learn, enjoy and achieve, and that my behaviour has an impact on this.

☐ I understand my strengths and the things that I find difficult, and I am happy to accept who I am – I am unique!

Session 1: Reputations, Exclusion, Behaviour and Me!

This first session begins by focusing students on auditing their behaviour and their relationships with their teachers across the curriculum. It is an important opportunity for students to stop and actually think about where their problems lie and where things are going well for them at the moment. This will act as a baseline for the programme, which will be measured again at the end.

The session then allows the facilitator to help students to begin to establish a more realistic picture of exclusion, reputations and behaviour through the use of a game. This game encourages students' own perceptions to be brought out into the open and, where necessary, questioned.

Secondary SEAL outcomes:

☐ I am beginning to know myself.

☐ I am working towards increasing my motivation to change my behaviour.

☐ I can communicate effectively with others, listening to what they say as well as expressing my own thoughts and views.

☐ I can work well in a group and co-operate with others.

☐ I am beginning to understand my responsibilities as a member of the school community.

Activity 1: Baseline – Lesson Audit

Preparation

☐ Print/photocopy the 'Baseline – Lesson Audit' worksheet for each student.

This audit is a crucial beginning to the programme. If preferred, you can complete it during the setting-up process when you meet each student individually to discuss the programme.

If this is the first session, however, read through the audit and ask the student to score each section out of 10 – 10 being the highest score and 0 being the lowest.

As a group, reflect on the differences between students' individual audits and ask students to look for patterns in their behaviour.

☐ Do they behave more positively with teachers with whom they have a better relationship?

☐ Is the subject they enjoy the least the one they struggle with?

- ☐ Is their poor behaviour linked to certain lessons?
- ☐ Where do most of their detentions come from, and why?
- ☐ Point out the differences, and ensure that they realise that they are doing well in certain areas of the curriculum.

Activity 2: Reputations, Behaviour and Me!

Preparation

- ☐ Print/photocopy and, if possible, laminate the 'Reputations, Exclusion, Behaviour and Me!' statements sheet. Cut out the statements to form individual cards.
- ☐ Print/photocopy the 'Agree', 'Disagree' and 'Not sure' sheets.

This is a simple activity which will help students to begin to think about some of the key aspects of exclusion and behaviour in general. Often students have an idea of what would happen and where they would go if they were permanently excluded, and what that actually means. However, in my experience their perception is often very different from the reality!

Each group member needs to take it in turns to take a card, read it out, think about it and then decide whether they 'agree', 'disagree' or are 'not sure' about the statement written on it.

Once a student has decided on whether they are going to place their card against the 'Agree', the 'Disagree' or the 'Not sure' sheet, use this opportunity to ask them why they think and feel that way. Do other students in the group agree or disagree?

The aim of this game is to get students talking and thinking; by the end of the game they will have a more accurate vision of exclusion, behaviour and themselves.

Activity 3: The Key Question is ...

Preparation

- ☐ Print/photocopy 'The Key Question Is ...' worksheet for each student.
- ☐ Print/photocopy the 'Answer ...' sheet for each student.
- ☐ Whiteboard or flipchart.

To end the session, hand out a copy of 'The Key Question Is...' worksheet to each student.

Ask each student to spend a few minutes making a list of what they think will be the greatest influence in their life over the next year.

Take feedback on their ideas and write this up on the whiteboard or flip chart.

The answer to the question is often a surprise! Hand out the 'Answer' sheet and discuss how, in fact, the students are in control of their own destiny and have the power to influence their own futures.

Baseline -- Lesson Audit

Name...   Date..

Lesson	Teacher	How much do I enjoy this lesson?	How good is my relationship with this teacher?	Can I do the work in class?	How do I behave in this class?

Reputations, Exclusion, Behaviour and Me!

Students often misbehave in lessons that they find difficult.
Explain your answer.

How you are feeling about school, home or friendships can affect how you behave in class.

When students get a reputation for being rude, difficult or challenging, it takes time and motivation to replace this reputation with a more positive one.

More girls than boys are permanently excluded in Britain each year.
Explain your answer.

Students who end up being permanently excluded from school don't achieve good GCSEs.

Students who blame everyone else for their actions will find it hard to make the changes they need to be able to stay in school.

Once you have a bad reputation, that's it – it sticks.

Getting excluded from school doesn't affect your chances of going to college.

Impressing other students around you is more important than doing as you are asked.

Students who are successful in changing their behaviour patterns have to be resilient. 'Resilient' means that when things go wrong, they bounce back and don't give up.

It's my behaviour, they're my choices and my actions … It's down to me.

If I am permanently excluded from school, I can choose where I go next.

Teachers often think badly of students who have a reputation, which is understandable.

The lessons students like, and in which they have a good relationship with the teacher, are usually the ones in which they behave well.

How we behave is a choice we have, regardless of what is going on around us.

P

DISAGREE

NOT SURE

The Key Question Is ...

What will be the greatest influence in your life over the next year?

Behaviour 4 My Future | 13

Answer ...

You will be the greatest influence in your life.

You have control.

The future doesn't just happen.

You can make a difference.

What does your future hold?

Session 2: My Future ... What Does It Hold?

For many students whose behaviour has resulted in exclusion from school, they are unable to link the 'here and now' with their future. This disaffection with their school, and with the long-term benefits of being at school, means that they are caught up in a cycle of negative thinking, feeling and behaviour. They are unaware of how the here and now will impact on their desired future.

This session has helped many students to make the link and to understand that, in reality, they will not be able to drive around in a flashy car, wearing the latest brand-name clothing, unless they take control and make better choices now.

Secondary SEAL outcomes:

☐ I am beginning to identify my current limitations and to develop the motivation to overcome them.

☐ I am starting to know myself and to develop an accurate picture of where I am.

☐ I am beginning to reflect on my actions.

☐ I am thinking about long-term rather than short-term benefits to education, and being able to delay gratification.

☐ I am starting to use my experiences, including mistakes and setbacks, to make appropriate changes to my plans and behaviour.

Activity 1: My Future ... What Does It Hold?

Preparation

☐ Print/photocopy the 'My Future ... What Does It Hold?' worksheet for each student.

☐ Whiteboard or flip chart.

This first activity allows students to think beyond school and imagine realistically what they would like in terms of cars, clothes, money, and so on, in the future.

Make sure that students keep this realistic – being a millionaire would be lovely, but is probably not a realistic preferred future!

When students have completed the activity, allow them to feed back as a group. On the whiteboard or flip chart, you could write up each heading from the worksheet, and add the students' names down the side, and as they call out their preferred futures, write these up for everyone to see.

Activity 2: My Here and Now

Preparation

☐   Print/photocopy the 'My Here and Now' worksheet for each student.

Having thought about where they would like to be in a few years' time, this activity links what is happening now and how it will affect the chances of that preferred future happening.

Ask each student to complete the activity. At the end of the worksheet they will be asked to set themselves a goal for the following week.

Ask each student to share their goals and the areas of their life which are currently affecting their ability to be successful in the future.

Be clear with the students that it is in their control to make changes, that they can overcome the obstacles, and that it is their level of motivation to do this that makes the difference.

It might be helpful to mention to students that Session 5 will be devoted to exploring what motivation is all about.

My Future ...
What Does It Hold?

In this exercise you need to imagine how you would like your life to be when you are 20 years old. Be realistic when answering the questions.

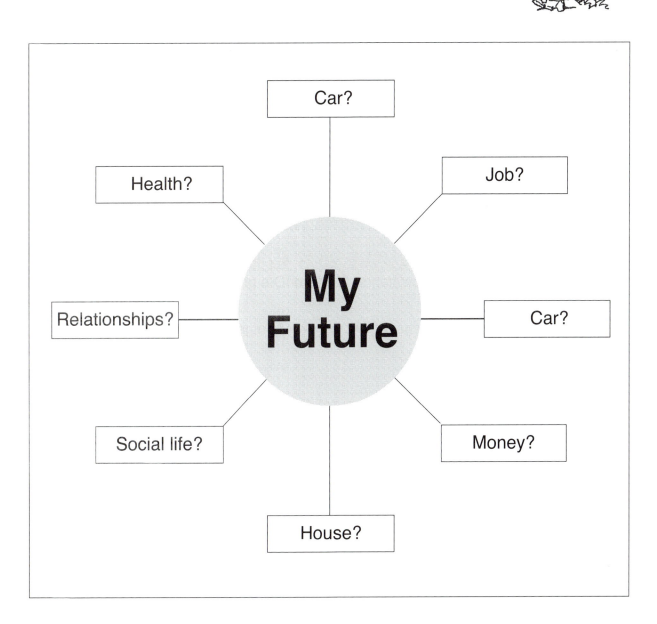

So, for each heading write a few lines about how you would like things to be for you.

Social life
_____
_____

Relationships
_____
_____

Health
_____
_____

Car
_____
_____

Job
_____
_____

Money
_____
_____

Clothes
_____
_____

House
_____

How does your preferred future look?
_____
_____

We'll talk the answers through as a group.
_____
_____

My Here and Now

In this exercise you need to be honest about what is going on now that could affect your preferred future. Have a look at these attitudes and problems:

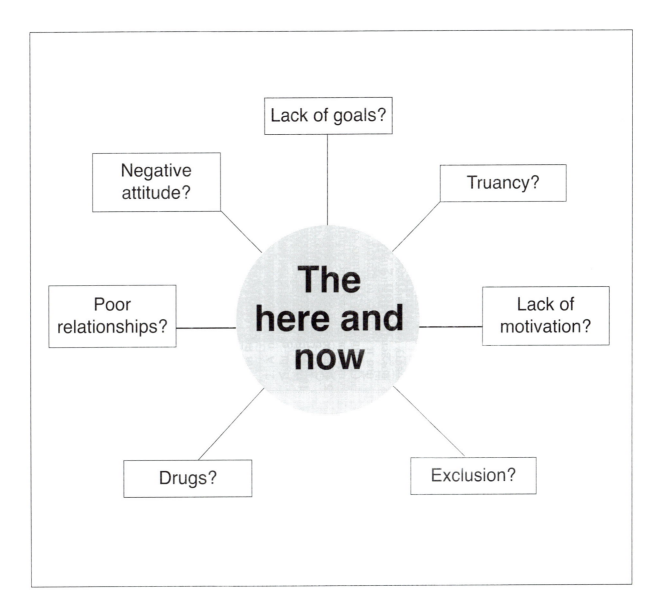

So, all these things will affect whether or not you achieve your preferred future. Be honest and write down the ones which, at the moment, could do this for you.

Drugs
_____

_____

Poor relationships
_____

_____

Negative attitude
_____

_____

Truancy
_____

_____

Lack of motivation
_____

_____

Exclusion
_____

_____

Lack of goals
_____

_____

Could these things affect your future? If so, how much?
0   1   2   3   4   5   6   7   8   9   10
Not at all   Really affect it

How motivated are you to make a difference?
0   1   2   3   4   5   6   7   8   9   10
Not at all   Really motivated

Do you have control over this?
0   1   2   3   4   5   6   7   8   9   10
Not at all   I'm in control

What is your goal for the next week?

_____

_____

_____

_____

Go for it!

Session 3: Thinking, Feeling and Behaviour

If you ask many students about how they feel in school, often they don't have the emotional vocabulary to express themselves. This session is designed to help such students to name those feelings and to understand how their thoughts and feelings are driving their behaviour.

It is an important session. Students need to be able to connect to how they feel, to stop and consider what is making them feel that way, and to acknowledge that they are not alone in carrying uncomfortable feelings around with them.

Secondary SEAL outcomes:

- ☐ I know and accept what I am feeling, and can label my feelings.
- ☐ I understand that the way I think affects the way I feel, and that the way I feel can affect the way I think, and I know that my thoughts and feelings influence my behaviour.
- ☐ I can use this knowledge and experience of how I think, feel and respond in order to manage my behaviour and build positive relationships with others.
- ☐ I can support others in my group who are experiencing personal problems.
- ☐ I can communicate effectively with others, listening to what others have to say, as well as expressing my own thoughts and feelings.
- ☐ I can work and learn in a group and co-operate well with others.

Activity 1: Search for the Feeling Words!

Preparation

- ☐ Print/photocopy the 'Search for the Feeling Words!' word search worksheet for each student.
- ☐ Whiteboard or flip chart.

This activity is a gentle introduction to feelings. First of all, ask the students to find as many words, which describe feelings, as possible from the chart. Time the word search, and then ask the students to write down on the sheet any feelings from the list that they experience.

If needed, prepare a further list of feelings on the whiteboard or flip chart for them to look at.

Talk through the range of feelings that they experience and how these feelings often overwhelm them and result in poor behaviour and negative consequences – detentions and exclusion. The key message is that many students experience uncomfortable feelings during a day at school: they are not alone.

Activity 2: My Feelings About My School

Preparation

☐ Print/photocopy the 'My Feelings About My School' worksheet for each student.

Ask students to complete the activity sheet 'My Feelings About My School', which asks them to focus on their six main feelings, why they feel that way and how these feelings can affect their behaviour.

Use the emotions word list to help students to complete the activity.

Take feedback from the group: it is an important learning outcome that students realise that their uncomfortable feelings are often shared by others.

Activity 3: Thinking, Feeling and Behaviour

Preparation

☐ Print/photocopy the 'Thinking, Feeling, Behaviour – Jack's Story' worksheet for each student.

☐ Whiteboard or flip chart.

Read through the example on the sheet of how Jack's thinking, feeling and behaviour linked together in school and resulted in regular problems.

Ask each student to think about and then share a situation in school in which this cycle has affected them. Write these up on the whiteboard or flipchart.

It is an important learning outcome that students understand that, in order to improve their situation at school, they have to be able to identify their feelings and thoughts, but to choose a behaviour which is positive.

Share some of your own experiences of how you have had to behave appropriately despite feeling bored or tense – for example, having to sit in a long meeting when you really have so much other work to do; or sitting a driving test and feeling stressed and thinking that you cannot go through with it.

Relate the cycle to famous people who have had to overcome negative thoughts and feelings in order to achieve their goals – for instance, athletes, sports personalities, and film stars.

Search for the Feeling Words!

How do you feel in school?

c	h	i	l	l	l	e	d	x	i	o	s	g	y	o	p
s	o	i	e	y	o	l	b	d	s	a	l	f	d	j
a	t	n	d	m	u	g	f	y	v	e	k	i	l	a
l	f	d	t	a	n	y	r	m	n	d	p	a	e	d
c	i	b	n	e	e	g	i	o	t	u	w	b	q	e
s	h	v	x	u	n	a	l	t	t	r	o	f	b	i
u	n	n	e	a	y	t	n	s	i	r	e	i	e	r
o	g	y	i	l	c	u	e	g	e	d	s	t	e	r
i	m	d	r	o	y	e	a	d	t	f	e	s	t	o
x	p	o	p	u	l	a	r	l	r	e	w	e	t	w
n	s	s	t	r	e	s	s	e	d	y	s	b	o	y
a	x	j	c	k	l	o	f	y	p	p	a	h	i	e
a	p	f	e	w	m	c	l	h	a	f	g	s	e	i
t	i	c	c	l	e	v	e	r	u	e	c	d	e	u
e	k	l	a	q	e	s	d	o	i	f	d	g	f	o
f	v	c	e	s	t	c	w	t	c	a	u	o	p	l
h	y	i	d	d	e	t	a	r	t	s	u	r	f	b

Angry
Contented
Frustrated
Bored
Anxious
Calm
Chilled
Happy
Lively
Safe
Lonely
Stressed
Worried
Clever
Stupid
Popular

Which feelings from the list do you experience during a school day?

-
-
-
-
-
-
-
-

My Feelings About My School?

With the help of the "Feelings" word list, think about and decide on at least 6 different feelings that you experience either in school, before you leave the house to come to school or when you leave school at the end of the day.

Feeling 1...............................

Why do you feel this way? What is happening? What thoughts are going through your head? How does this affect the way you act?

....

....

....

....

....

Feeling 2...............................

Why do you feel this way? What is happening? What thoughts are going through your head? How does this affect the way you act?

....

....

....

....

....

Feeling 3.............................

Why do you feel this way? What is happening? What thoughts are going through your head? How does this affect the way you act?

....

....

....

....

....

Feeling 4………………………..

Why do you feel this way? What is happening? What thoughts are going through your head? How does this affect the way you act?

....

....

....

....

....

Feeling 5……………………..

Why do you feel this way? What is happening? What thoughts are going through your head? How does this affect the way you act?

....

....

....

....

....

Feeling 6…………………..

Why do you feel this way? What is happening? What thoughts are going through your head? How does this affect the way you act?

....

....

....

....

....

Listen to other students' feelings. Do we all feel the same or are we all carrying around different emotional baggage?

How you feel about something… will affect the way you think. And if you let it, it will affect the way you behave… truancy.

Angry	Anxious	Lively	Worried
Contented	Calm	Safe	Clever
Frustrated	Chilled	Lonely	Stupid
Bored	Happy	Stressed	Popular

Thinking, Feeling and Behaviour – Jack's Story

Jack is a Year 9 student who is on Stage B of the Schools Exclusion Stages. He has a history of difficult and challenging behaviour in certain subjects. He likes practical subjects, such as Art, Design and Technology, and ICT. His behaviour is difficult in lessons that he finds hard, such as English, French and History – in these lessons he has to do a lot of writing, which he doesn't enjoy. He feels stupid in these lessons; he doesn't understand the work and so he finds a way to avoid doing it.

When Jack is in a French lesson this is his 'thinking, feeling and behaviour' cycle.

Jack's thinking ... I don't want to be here. I can't do the work. I find English hard enough and I have to try to learn French. If I put my hand up and ask for help it will be embarrassing.

Jack's feelings ... Stressed, anxious, bored, worried about having to do the work.

Jack's behaviour ... Out of seat, turning round to chat and distract others, shouting out and refusing to complete the work; avoiding the fact that he finds it hard.

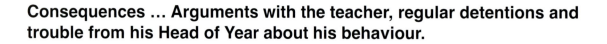

Consequences ... Arguments with the teacher, regular detentions and trouble from his Head of Year about his behaviour.

Session 4: What Affects How I Feel About School?

Having identified the feelings they experience and how these can impact on their behaviour, this session moves students on to identify what affects the way they feel, the influences on their behaviour, and how they can reduce these and manage themselves effectively.

Students will be encouraged to solve their problems rather than allow them to weigh them down, and give up – this pessimistic attitude needs to be challenged.

Secondary SEAL outcomes:

☐ I can begin to recognise conflicting emotions and manage them in ways that are positive.

☐ I can use my knowledge of how I think and feel in order to respond appropriately and choose my own behaviour.

☐ I can choose to direct my attention and resist distractions.

☐ I can set myself goals and challenges and celebrate when I achieve them.

☐ I can work around potential obstacles.

☐ I know how to bring about change in myself and others.

☐ I can communicate effectively with others.

☐ I can work well in a group and co-operate with others.

☐ I can begin to achieve a level of independence from others in order to improve my behaviour.

☐ I can use a range of strategies to solve problems, and monitor the effectiveness of them to help me plan my behaviour.

Activity 1: What Affects How I Feel About School?

Preparation

☐ Print/photocopy the 'What Affects How I Feel About School?' worksheet for each student.

Introduce the session by talking about the range of situations that can affect how we feel. Perhaps a student is having problems at home, perhaps they are not getting on so well with other students, or maybe they are thinking negatively about the situation they are in, and can't see a way forward. The activity sheet contains a range of examples given by other students. Read through each one as a group and ask students to tick those which they think affect them the most.

Activity 2: Face the Problem and Solve It!

Preparation

☐ Print/photocopy the 'Face the Problem and Solve It!' worksheet containing the blank 'wall', for each student; enlarge it to A3 if possible.

☐ Print/photocopy the completed example of the 'Face the Problem and Solve It!' worksheet to be shown to students before they do the activity, and for use during any feedback discussion.

☐ Whiteboard or flip chart.

Following on from the first activity in this session, this next activity asks students to look again at the 'What Affects How I Feel About School?' worksheet from the first activity, but to take the exercise one step further. Read through the examples again as a group, but this time ask students to choose just one example that applies to them. Then ask them to write on the wall on their 'Face the Problem and Solve It!' worksheet, a range of strategies they could use to overcome this influence on their feelings.

Give students 10 minutes to carry out this activity.

☐ What strategies could they use to overcome the problem?

☐ How do they need to think?

☐ Who may need to help them?

☐ Is there something they need to do differently?

If needed, work through one example on the whiteboard or flip chart as a group. The completed example of the 'Face the Problem and Solve It!' worksheet has been provided for you to use during this feedback discussion. Ask students to share their walls and the strategies they have identified. Allow other students to give feedback.

What Affects How I Feel About School?

The teachers don't like me

I've got a reputation

My thinking is all negative

I find some of the lessons boring

I don't think I can change

I lack confidence in myself

All my mates get into trouble, what will happen if I am good?

My mates expect me to be like this

I don't feel good at anything

I don't understand a lot of the work

I don't see the point

My health

I don't have a goal for the future

I've got so much going on outside of school

Stuff going on at home

Problems with other students

Face the Problem and Solve It!
Example

Drink water not coke

Eat Breakfast!

Eat healthier food

Take some lunch to school

My Health?

Get up earlier to have breakfast - set alarm clock

Ask mum to get me some cereal I like

Face the Problem and Solve It!

Session 5: What's Motivation All About?

Without motivation, long-term behaviour change is unlikely to be seen. Many disaffected students have, in effect, given up and have little or no motivation to succeed. An important ingredient in any emotional literacy programme aimed at this cohort of students is that they begin to feel motivated to improve. This section also introduces students to the need for them to be intrinsically motivated: it is not ideal for any student to make changes to their behaviour only because they have been promised a reward. Students who are subject to this external locus of control are unlikely to maintain positive changes once the rewards stop flowing.

Secondary SEAL outcomes:

- ☐ I understand why I need to feel motivated to achieve.
- ☐ I understand that I need motivation to bring about change in myself.
- ☐ I can communicate effectively with others.
- ☐ I can work well in a group and co-operate with others.
- ☐ I can begin to achieve a level of independence from others to improve my behaviour.

Activity 1: What's Motivation All About?

Preparation

- ☐ Print/photocopy the 'What's Motivation All About?' worksheet for each student.
- ☐ Whiteboard or flip chart.

Start the activity by asking students the following questions:

- ☐ What does feeling motivated mean?
- ☐ Is it important?
- ☐ Can they think of any film stars or sports personalities who need to be motivated?
- ☐ Why do they think these people need to be motivated?

Write up their ideas on the whiteboard or flip chart.

Hand out a copy of the worksheet and read it to the group. This sheet is an easy-to-grasp explanation of what motivation is – that is, it is the key to their success.

Ask each student to share how motivated they are to improve their behaviour. Make sure the answers are recorded on their sheets for future reference.

Activity 2: So … What's It Going to Take to Motivate You?

Preparation

☐ Print/photocopy the 'So … What's It Going to Take to Motivate You …?' worksheet for each student.

☐ Whiteboard or flip chart.

Write the following two headings on the board or flip chart:

1. Benefits of poor behaviour
2. Benefits of good behaviour

Ask students to brainstorm ideas for each heading, and write these ideas up. There are some short-term benefits that students often raise, for example, with regard to the benefits of poor behaviour – fitting in with others, being part of the 'in' crowd, gaining peer group respect. Make sure you point out that these are short term: if a student is permanently excluded from school, everyone else in the class will still be there!

Hand out the 'So … What's It Going to Take to Motivate You …?' worksheet.

Ask students if they have ever made improvements because their parents or school have offered them a reward? Share experiences within the group. Introduce the concept of internal and external locus of control. Students who rely on rewards to improve their behaviour are externally motivated – the key message for them is that they have to be internally motivated.

Read through the statements made by students about the benefits of better behaviour, and ask students to tick the statements with which they identify. How would they feel if they were one of those students who made these statements?

What's MOTIVATION All About?

What motivates you?

Think about this …

… You have been given a gorgeous shiny blue SUBURU IMPREZA WRX!!! It has just had a full service, and it has a shiny set of alloys; it's polished and ready to go. This car is apparently the business! It has great potential. (Sound familiar?)

BUT … It isn't going anywhere.

WHY? Well, until someone sits behind the wheel, puts the key in and starts it up, it just doesn't work, does it?

What's the key?
The Key is MOTIVATION.

Have you got any?

Out of 10 – 10 being the highest score – how motivated are you to improve your behaviour?

So ... What's It Going to Take to MOTIVATE You to Avoid Exclusion and Have a Better Future?

If you are the type of student who has managed to make changes to your behaviour before because you were promised a new Ipod® or PS3®, then it is unlikely that you kept up with the improvements once the rewards stopped!

To really make a long-term difference, your motivation needs to come from within you! Then we will really see progress!

Here are some benefits of better behaviour, which other students, who were in your position, talked about. Tick the ones that you think would be beneficial for you.

- ☐ I am getting along much better with my teachers now.

- ☐ It's a relief to not have so many hours of detentions every week; I can go straight out of school and see my mates.

- ☐ I got really fed up with always being sent to the Head of Year; now he tells me how well I'm doing and I don't dread seeing him!

- ☐ My parents were really stressy, they always had phone calls and letters every week asking them to go to meetings. Getting on better at school has really helped the atmosphere at home.

- ☐ Some of the teachers with whom I wasn't getting along before are really OK, and now that I'm not disrupting their lesson every week, they are interested in me for the right reasons.

- ☐ It felt like such an uphill struggle to start with; now I am on track for my GCSEs and I'm going out to college every week. I feel so much happier now that I've sorted myself out.

Session 6: What Can Affect My Motivation?

This session moves on to support students in overcoming some of the factors that can affect their level of motivation. Some of these factors are directly related to them: the way they think about a situation, or the result of having an unhealthy diet. Others are linked to how secure they feel and whether or not they have a strong sense of belonging to the school itself. Having identified the sources of their demotivators, students will move on to identify positive steps they can take to reduce these demotivators. The need to be a resilient learner is introduced during this session.

Secondary SEAL outcomes:

☐ I can plan and work around or overcome potential obstacles.

☐ I understand how my thoughts and feelings can influence my behaviour.

☐ I can think about uncomfortable feelings I have and consider a range of strategies to reduce or manage them.

☐ I can begin to understand how setting goals and challenges for myself increases my level of motivation.

☐ I can communicate effectively with others, listening to what others have to say as well as expressing my own thoughts and feelings.

☐ I can work well in groups.

☐ I can begin to develop a range of strategies to solve problems that I have.

☐ I can begin to think about how to repair damaged relationships.

Activity 1: What Can Affect My Motivation?

Preparation

☐ Print/photocopy the 'What Can Affect My Motivation?' worksheet for each student.

☐ Print/photocopy the poster 'Get Your Head in the Right Place' for each student.

☐ A3 paper for each student and a selection of coloured pens.

Read through the worksheet and ask students to tick the factors which affect their levels of motivation. Then move on to ask students to identify the three main demotivators on their list and to think about how they can improve the situation or overcome the obstacle.

Alternatively, ask each student to choose one factor and design a poster to illustrate how they are going to change the situation. The demotivator should be written in the centre of the page and the list of strategies written around the outside, in the way illustrated on the following page.

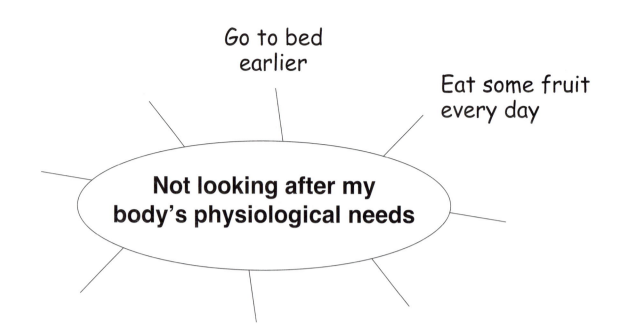

Go to bed earlier

Eat some fruit every day

Not looking after my body's physiological needs

To close the session, hand out the poster 'Get Your Head in the Right Place'. This is a humourous way of helping students to realise that the way they are thinking about the situation at school really matters. Positive thinking is crucial.

What Can Affect My Motivation?

There are many things that can affect your level of motivation. Some of these are 'intrinsic' – within you. Others are 'extrinsic' – factors which are outside and around you.

At this point, you need to think about what has prevented you from moving forward and making the changes you need to make in order to improve both your time at school and your future.

Tick any of the following questions which you recognise as being a demotivator.

☐   Do you look after your body's physiological needs? Are you eating properly? Do you drink enough water for your brain and body to be able to function properly?

☐   Do you feel safe here in school? Is home a safe place for you to be?

☐   Do you have good feelings about school? Do you feel as though you are part of the school community and that you belong?

☐   Are you told when to do things the right way at home or school?

☐   Do you get recognition for your achievements?

☐   Is the way you are thinking about the problem affecting the way you feel and behave?

☐   Are you able to do the work in class? Are there subjects that you find hard?

☐   Do you have good relationships with some teachers?

☐   Are you drifting along in school without really thinking about where you are heading?

☐   Is how you are feeling and thinking about the situation affecting your motivation?

Make a list of the three most significant demotivators you are aware of, and think about how you can let go of these and increase your motivation at the same time. Perhaps you need help, or perhaps it's down to you to make the changes you need to make in order to move on?

_____

_____

_____

_____

_____

Remember … the best way to deal with a problem is to solve it!

Get Your Head in the Right Place

One of the most important things that you need to do if you want to change your behaviour is …

… get your head in the right place!

Session 7: Goal Setting

Frequently, students whose behaviour is difficult at school fail to see the longer term goals that education has to offer them. Without a goal – something to reach for and motivate them – behaviour change can be hard. This session allows students to understand the importance of goal setting, and to think about the steps that are involved in achieving an overall goal.

Secondary SEAL outcomes:

- ☐ I can begin to understand how setting goals and challenges for myself increases my level of motivation.
- ☐ I can set goals and challenges for myself.
- ☐ I can break a longer term plan into small, achievable steps.
- ☐ I know how to bring about change in myself.
- ☐ I understand that I can learn from my mistakes and bounce back from disappointment or failure.
- ☐ I can communicate effectively with others, listening to what others have to say, as well as expressing my own thoughts and feelings.
- ☐ I can work well in groups.

Activity 1: Goal Setting

Preparation

- ☐ Print/photocopy the 'Goal Setting' and 'My Goal for this School Year' worksheets for each student.
- ☐ Whiteboard or flip chart.

Start the session by writing up on a board or flip chart the word 'Goals'.

Ask the group:

- ☐ What is a goal?
- ☐ Why do they think it is important to have one?
- ☐ Do they have a goal?
- ☐ What do they think their parents' goals are for them?

Hand out the first worksheet and read through it as a group. This is a humorous way of explaining goals and how, without one, they are simply drifting along.

- ☐ Can students think about any famous people who set themselves goals?
- ☐ Do we achieve goals straight away?
- ☐ How do we achieve them – one step at a time?

Use the following example, if needed, to explain how someone famous achieved their goals.

Did David Beckham wake up one morning as a famous and wealthy football star? No!

He set himself a goal early in life. He wanted to play football for Manchester United, but he knew that in order to achieve that, he would have to work towards it step by step. So, he joined a football club, he practised hard, often missing out on other stuff that his friends did, such as going out to parties or youth club events. He needed to be resilient; it wouldn't always have gone well – he probably had days when he really felt he wouldn't get there – but he didn't let himself dwell on those negative thoughts for too long. He picked himself up and got on with taking the steps towards his goal. Eventually, his persistence, resilience and motivation got him what he wanted – and look at him now!

That's how you achieve a goal. What is yours going to be?

Ask each student to write down a goal for the year on the worksheet provided. The illustration on this sheet shows lower level needs leading to self-actualisation – in this instance, a small step needed to work towards an overall goal. Students start at the bottom, identifying the first step towards their goal, then the next step and then the overall goal for the school year. Make sure they think about how they will feel when they achieve it.

Ask each student to read out their steps towards their overall end-of-year goal.

Activity 2: Top Tips for Achieving Your Goal

Preparation

☐   Print/photocopy the 'Top Tips for Achieving Your Goal' worksheet for each student.

☐   Whiteboard or flipchart.

This is a list of tips for students to think about when they are reaching for their goal. You can write these up on a board or flip chart and talk through them one by one, or hand out the sheet and ask a student to read out the tips to everyone.

Finally, reflect on the quotation at the bottom of the worksheet – motivate students to start to achieve their goal for the next week!

Goal Setting

Why is it important to set goals?

It's important in terms of **motivation** and **success**. If you were to ask any famous person – Eminem, Madonna, Wayne Rooney, Michael Schumacher – what motivates them, they would say that it is reaching and achieving their goals.

So … Do you have a goal?

If you have no goals for your future, then you are just a 'passenger' – you're not in control. You're just drifting along.

Do something about it!

'If you don't know where you are going, you'll end up someplace else.'

(Yogi Berra)

Session 8: Getting a Grip on My Anger

We know that getting angry in school often leads to confrontation, conflict and exclusion. The sessions that follow are designed to help students to recognise when they are starting to feel angry, to identify why they are feeling angry, and then to manage that feeling effectively and so reduce the negative outcomes for themselves.

Secondary SEAL outcomes:

- ☐ I understand why feelings sometimes take over or get out of control.

- ☐ I know what makes me feel angry.

- ☐ I have a range of strategies for managing my anger so that I do not behave in a way that has negative consequences for me or for other people.

- ☐ I can communicate effectively with others, listening to what others have to say, as well as expressing my own thoughts and feelings.

- ☐ I can work well in groups.

Activity 1: Getting a Grip on My Anger – My Self-assessment

Preparation

- ☐ Print/photocopy the 'Getting a Grip on My Anger' worksheet sheet for each student.

    Print/photocopy the 'Managing My Anger Self-assessment' worksheet for each student.

- ☐ Whiteboard or flip chart.

Write up on a board or flip chart the three quotations from the worksheet, so that students are able to see them.

Ask students if they agree with what these other students have said – is this how they also feel and behave?

Hand out the worksheet and read it through as a group. Emphasise to students that finding a way of managing their anger is an important skill for life, not just for school.

Ask students to complete the self-assessment. This easy-to-use assessment will help you and the students to identify areas of strength and weakness in this personal competency. Ask students for feedback on their self-assessments.

What is Anger Anyway?

Imagine you are angry:

Your heart is beating so quickly.

Your head is in a spin.

Your muscles are tense.

You have clenched fists.

Your stomach tightens.

You are hot.

You are heading out of control
– towards an 'emotional hijack'.

This is your body's response to what it thinks is a threat.

The part of your brain which manages emotions has hijacked the part of your brain which does all your thinking. You are not thinking clearly any more.

It is a really intense and uncomfortable feeling.

Perhaps your first reaction is to lash out at someone or something?

The Anger Perception Game – Statements

- ☐ A physical symptom which indicates that you are getting angry is that your heart starts beating really quickly.

- ☐ You can think perfectly clearly when you are at the peak of anger.

- ☐ Talking to yourself – self-talk – can help to calm you down.

- ☐ Getting angry can be a good thing.

- ☐ Adrenalin is a hormone that the body releases when you are angry or scared.

- ☐ Listening to music doesn't help our mood.

- ☐ Taking exercise is a good anger buster.

- ☐ It is impossible to deal with anger and take control.

- ☐ Families often feel ashamed when their children get angry and hurt other people with unkind words or actions.

- ☐ Getting angry and 'letting it all out' feels good, but it only feels good for a short time.

- ☐ Taking deep breaths will help to calm you down.

- ☐ Getting angry at school is a common feeling.

- ☐ No one has the right to be violent.

- ☐ Students who have a reputation for getting angry are popular at school.

- ☐ Adults can manage their anger much better than children and young people.

- ☐ Having a laugh could help you calm down.

- ☐ Teachers find it easy to control their anger in class.

- ☐ Counting to 10 will give you time to calm down and make a better choice.

- ☐ Our brains control our responses.

- ☐ Going to prison is a long-term consequence of getting angry all the time and hurting people.

- ☐ Some students just can't help getting angry.

- ☐ The main reason for exclusion from school is related to getting angry.

- ☐ It wouldn't help to go and talk to someone.

- ☐ Anger builds up inside us and something little often pushes us over the edge – we have an angry outburst.

- ☐ There aren't any benefits to be gained from learning to manage our anger.

- ☐ Students often feel guilty and regret their actions once they have calmed down.

People Who Fly into a Rage

People who fly into a rage will always crash land!

Session 9: Triggers and Chillers!

Having introduced the emotion of anger and the body's physiological responses to it, this session supports students in identifying their personal anger triggers. This identification is an important step in the process of learning to manage their anger.

Students will then progress to thinking about a range of anger blockers that they can begin to use in order to calm themselves down and avoid reaching the peak of anger.

Secondary SEAL outcomes:

- ☐ I understand why feelings sometimes take over or get out of control.
- ☐ I know what makes me feel angry.
- ☐ I have a range of strategies for managing my anger so that I do not behave in a way that has negative consequences for me or for other people.
- ☐ I can communicate effectively with others, listening to what others have to say, as well as expressing my own thoughts and feelings.
- ☐ I can work well in groups.

Activity 1: What Makes You Angry?

Preparation

- ☐ Print/photocopy the 'What Makes You Angry?' worksheet for each student.
- ☐ Whiteboard or flip chart.

Write this heading up on a board or flipchart: What makes you angry?

Ask students to come up with their personal anger triggers, and then write these up on the board. It is useful to comment on the range of triggers – how 'being shouted at', for example, may make one student angry, whereas another student doesn't find it a real trigger situation.

Ask students to complete the checklist on the worksheet by scoring each trigger situation out of a possible 10 – 1 being a low trigger through to 10 being a very high trigger.

Take feedback from the students on their trigger identification.

Changing the way students deal with their anger is paramount. Getting angry, losing control and shouting, swearing, throwing things or lashing out leads to exclusion.

Introduce the next activity, which supports students in developing a new range of strategies for avoiding the emotional hijack associated with anger.

Activity 2: Take Control and Chill Out!

Preparation

☐   Print/photocopy the 'Take Control and Chill Out!' worksheet for each student.

Read through the suggestions on the worksheet. These are tried-and-tested anger blockers that other students have used successfully. Ask students to choose a selection that they think may work for them.

Students need to commit to try these out at school or home over the coming weeks. It is important to explain to students that changing their automatic reactions – shouting, swearing or lashing out – will take time. At the moment, these are their learned behaviours: their brain will just do this without thinking about the consequences! Learning a new way of reacting will take practice before they get it right on every occasion. Remind them that they didn't learn to ride a bike the first time they jumped on one; they got on, fell off, got on, fell off, wobbled a bit, fell off, and so on and so on, until their brain made all the right connections and off they went!

Activity 3: The Management Recipe!

Preparation

☐   Print/photocopy 'The Management Recipe!' worksheet for each student.

☐   Whiteboard or flip chart.

Often students are told to count to 10 when they get angry, but many students have told me that this just doesn't work! The point of counting to 10 is to buy them some time to think: this is the first ingredient in the 'The Management Recipe!'

Write up on a board or flip chart 'Anger is only one letter short of _anger', and ask students to try to work out what the missing letter is.

It is 'D' for DANGER!

Close the session by handing each student a copy of the worksheet 'The Management Recipe!' Read this through with the students.

What Makes You Angry?

We are all different. Different things spark us off. Our past experiences often trick our brains into action. Often we react to situations that aren't a threat to us really, but the primitive response of 'flight or fight' kicks in and off we go.

Have a look at the following list. Do any of these things do it for you?

Score out of 10

Being called names ....

Being insulted ....

Feeling that you are in danger ....

Feeling picked on...

Getting the blame when it wasn't you ....

Someone being rude about your family ....

Bullying ....

Not being listened to ....

Getting no attention ....

Injustice..

Not being respected...

Being lied to ....

Not getting your own way ....

Someone breaking your stuff...

Someone telling a secret that you told them...................................

Session 10: Stressed Out!

Stress can be a harmful feeling if we allow it to go unchecked and affect our behaviour. All of us will feel stress at some time during our lives; how we cope and reduce that feeling is the focus of this session.

In school there are many situations which stress students. Some of these are related to being in certain lessons, whereas others may be related to times in the school year when exams have to be taken.

This session begins by supporting students in identifying the potential stress factors around them, and then moves on to share strategies for coping with stress and for preventing it from becoming overwhelming.

Secondary SEAL outcomes:

- ☐ I know what makes me feel stressed.
- ☐ I have a range of strategies for managing my stress and reducing the physical and emotional symptoms related to it.
- ☐ I can communicate effectively with others, listening to what they have to say, as well as expressing my own thoughts and views.
- ☐ I can work well in groups.
- ☐ I can empathise with other students who find different situations stressful in their lives.

Activity 1: Feeling Stressed

Preparation

- ☐ Print/photocopy the 'Feeling Stressed' worksheet for each student.
- ☐ Whiteboard or flip chart.

Introduce the feeling of stress to students by writing 'Feeling stressed' on the board, and asking them the following questions:

- ☐ How would they describe stress?
- ☐ What do they think stresses their parents?
- ☐ What do they think stresses their teachers?
- ☐ Does feeling stressed affect people's behaviour?

Hand out the 'Feeling Stressed' worksheet to each student and ask one of the students to read through the examples of different situations that typically stress students. Students should tick the situations which have in the past caused them to feel stress.

Activity 2: Symptoms of Stress

Preparation

☐ Print/photocopy the two worksheets 'Emotional Symptoms of Stress' and 'Physical Symptoms of Stress' for each student.

☐ Whiteboard or flip chart.

Moving on from considering what makes them feel stressed, students will now begin to consider how the feeling of stress affects their emotional and physical health.

Ask students, one at a time, to think about an emotional symptom of stress and share this with the rest of the group.

Then ask students, again one at a time, to think about a physical symptom of stress and share this with the rest of the group.

Write their ideas on the board or flipchart.

Hand out the worksheets and read, one by one, the symptoms listed on them. Ask students to identify from these the emotional and physical symptoms that they themselves may have experienced. For now, they should do this silently, keeping their thoughts to themselves.

If you feel that the group has the confidence to do so, it would be desirable for students then to share with each other the symptoms they have individually identified.

Activity 3: Strategies for Managing that Stress!

Preparation

☐ Print/photocopy the two worksheets 'Strategies for Managing that Stress' and 'Top Tips for Coping with that Stress' for each student.

Once we have recognised that we are feeling stressed, we need to think about how we can reduce the feeling and get ourselves back on track. Sometimes this might be as simple as sharing our feelings with a close friend.

Ask students to complete the 'Strategies for Managing that Stress' worksheet. This gives a list of 11 suggested ideas or strategies, each of which they need to score according to whether they always, sometimes or never adopt it.

Once the students have completed the worksheet, take feedback from the group on each idea. Ask them who tries that idea already? Who might give it a try from now on?

To close the session, hand out a copy of the second worksheet 'Top Tips for Coping with that Stress'.

Ask one of the students to read through this worksheet.

Always be prepared to share an experience of your own – a time when you felt stressed and how you coped.

Feeling Stressed

What is Stress?

You have probably heard people say they are stressed, but do you know what it actually means?

One way of explaining stress is by saying that it refers to a situation which makes you feel anxious or worried, sad or angry, or a mixture of all those feelings.

What Stresses Students Out?

☐ Not understanding the work in class.

☐ Feeling under pressure when coursework starts to pile up.

☐ Having problems in school with other students.

☐ Being bullied.

☐ Not getting on well with a particular teacher.

☐ Arguments with people at home – parents or siblings.

☐ Having too much homework.

Tick any of the above that could be stress factors for you.

Are there any more you could add?

Emotional Symptoms of STRESS

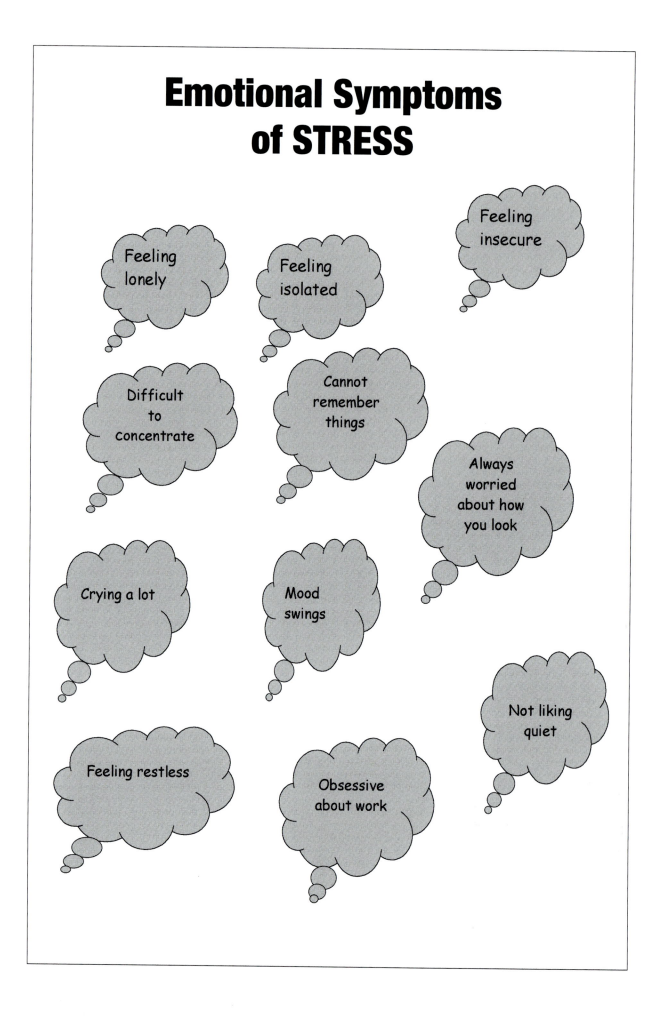

Physical Symptoms of STRESS

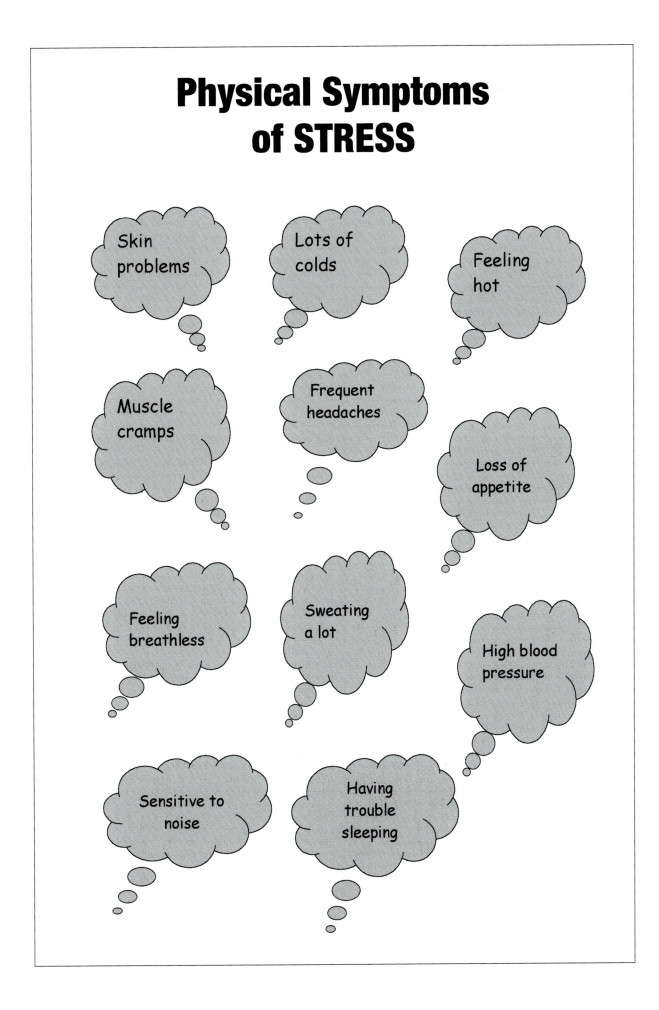

Strategies for Managing that STRESS

It is important that you develop a range of strategies for taking control of stress and reducing the feeling of it, so that you can function well. At the moment, what do you do to help yourself?

	Always	Sometimes	Never
I have a hobby or interest that I do regularly out of school.			
I always go and talk to someone if I am feeling stressed.			
I try to have a laugh and some fun.			
I am good at expressing my feelings to others.			
I have at least one good friend I will talk to.			
I try to manage my time as well as I can.			
I take some kind of energetic exercise each week.			
I chill out after a difficult day and watch TV, or play my favourite music.			
I treat myself sometimes to a favourite magazine or CD.			
I am good at giving people affection and I am good at receiving it.			
If I need to, I will go and have some quiet time on my own.			

Top Tips for Coping with that STRESS

First of all go and talk to someone!

A teacher, a close friend, the school nurse, your doctor or your parents – all of these people can help you.

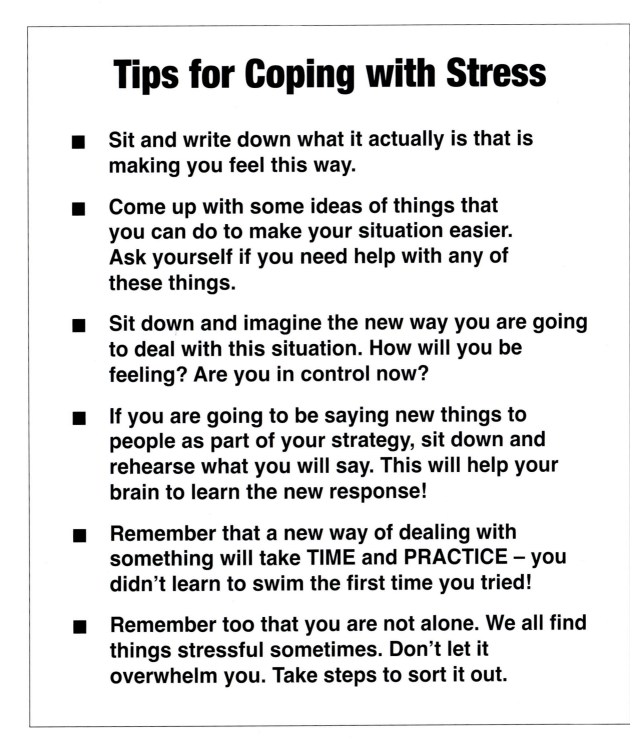

Tips for Coping with Stress

- Sit and write down what it actually is that is making you feel this way.

- Come up with some ideas of things that you can do to make your situation easier. Ask yourself if you need help with any of these things.

- Sit down and imagine the new way you are going to deal with this situation. How will you be feeling? Are you in control now?

- If you are going to be saying new things to people as part of your strategy, sit down and rehearse what you will say. This will help your brain to learn the new response!

- Remember that a new way of dealing with something will take TIME and PRACTICE – you didn't learn to swim the first time you tried!

- Remember too that you are not alone. We all find things stressful sometimes. Don't let it overwhelm you. Take steps to sort it out.

Session 11: Surviving the Classroom

Throughout each student's time at school they will encounter a range of situations in which they need to make the right choice with regard to how they behave. Unfortunately, some students have only a limited range of responses and many of these lead them into conflict. This session involves students in identifying positive responses to everyday situations through a game which also allows the facilitator an opportunity to question the consequences of some of their current responses.

Secondary SEAL outcomes:

☐ I can communicate effectively with others, listening to what others have to say, as well as expressing my own thoughts and feelings.

☐ I can work well in groups.

☐ I can identify my current limitations and feel positive about them.

☐ I can reflect on my actions and identify lessons to be learned from them.

☐ I can choose from a range of responses for managing impulses and strong emotions so they do not lead me to behave in ways that would have negative consequences for me or for other people.

Activity 1: Surviving the Classroom

Preparation

☐ Print/photocopy and, if possible, laminate the 'Surviving the Classroom' cards and cut them out for the game.

☐ Print/photocopy and, if possible, laminate the response cards, cut them out and spread them out on a table.

Each student takes it in turns to take a 'Surviving the Classroom' card. They must read out the card and then choose a response card. Encourage students to share why they have chosen the particular response card they have, and what the outcome of that response would be for them. Is it a response that they currently use, or one they need to learn and try out? Deliberately, there are some cards that don't have appropriate responses: this is to encourage students to start to think for themselves about a strategy that would best fit the situation. If a student can't find an appropriate response card, ask them to tell the group what they would do.

Surviving the Classroom

The teacher shouts at you across the room in front of everyone else.
You feel embarrassed.

You arrive late to the class again and the lesson has started.

You are caught truanting and are in trouble.

The teacher won't let you go out of the lesson to the toilet and
you are desperate.

You are caught smoking in the toilets.

A friend asks you for help in the lesson and you are accused of chatting.

You get excluded for swearing at a teacher.

You can't do the work in class.

You get the blame for throwing a pen across the room,
but it wasn't you.

You don't get on very well with the teacher because of your previous disruptive behaviour.

You are getting bullied in school.

You are told to sit by someone whom you know will distract you.

You are asked to wait outside the classroom because you will not stop chattering while the teacher is giving the class instructions.

Another student has sent you a note in class containing a nasty remark, and you are feeling wound up about it.

The student behind you keeps making remarks about you under his breath each time the teacher is out of earshot.

You arrive at your lesson and the teacher is a cover teacher. All the other students are saying that they are going to play up.

A boy or girl you fancy asks you to throw them a rubber across the room.

Surviving the Classroom – Response Cards

I will stop and think carefully about how I respond.	I need to take better care of myself.	I will truant.
I will walk away.	I will shout.	I will hit them.
I will ask for some help.	I will talk calmly about it.	It's just me, it's my fault.
I won't talk to anyone.	I'll act stupid to avoid the problem.	I will just ignore it.
I need to remember it's just one lesson.	I need to improve, so I'm not going to blow it now – just do as I am asked and talk about it later after class.	I will just give up.
I will think positively about myself.	I've made a mistake, but I can get better.	I really need to talk to someone about how I feel. I'm finding school tough.

Session 12: Multiple Intelligences – What's It All About?

A very common feeling among disaffected students is that of failure. Their perception is that they are 'stupid' or 'no good' at school. Often this has more to do with teaching and learning styles that don't engage them positively in the lesson, coupled with a lack of self-belief. Understanding that there is more than one way to be intelligent provides a huge self-esteem boost to students who currently don't feel that they are successful learners. This session focuses students on profiling where their natural intelligences lie, and relating these to their strengths within the National Curriculum.

Secondary SEAL outcomes:

☐ I can communicate effectively with others, listening to what others have to say, as well as expressing my own thoughts and feelings.

☐ I can work well in groups.

☐ I can identify my current limitations and feel positive about them.

☐ I can identify my strengths and feel positive about them.

☐ I know that I am a unique individual.

Activity 1: Multiple Intelligences – What's It All About?

Preparation

☐ Print/photocopy the 'Multiple Intelligences – What's It All About?' worksheet for each student.

As a group, read through the explanation of multiple intelligences and the eight different ways to be intelligent according to Howard Gardner (1993), as given on the 'Multiple Intelligences – What's It All About?' worksheet.

Activity 2: What Kind of Intelligences Do They Have?

Preparation

☐ Print/photocopy the 'Famous People – What Kind of Intelligences Do They Have?' worksheet for each student.

☐ Whiteboard or flip chart.

Gardner, H. (1993) *Frames of Mind: The Theory of Multiple Intelligences* (2nd edn), Fontana, London. (First published in 1983 by Basic Books, New York.)

This is an exercise which asks students to consider the types of intelligence that famous people have. Allow students to look through the explanations given in Activity 1 as they complete the task.

As an alternative, you might choose to write up on the whiteboard or flip chart either the names of the famous people listed on the 'Famous People – What Kind of Intelligences Do They Have?' worksheet, or the names of other famous people. Ask the students for ideas of names to include and complete the exercise as a group.

Activity 3: My Multiple Intelligence Profile

Preparation

- [ ] Print/photocopy the 'My Multiple Intelligence Profile' worksheets for each student.

- [ ] Whiteboard or flip chart.

This is an easy-to-use profile whereby students can assess their own natural intelligences. Ask each student to complete it.

Write the headings of the eight different intelligences up on a board or flipchart, and ask each student to come up to the board and write their name under the intelligences that they have discovered they have.

Remind students that their combination is unique to them, and throughout their lives some of these will be enhanced, while others will fade away and new skills and interests will take their place.

- [ ] Are there any surprises?
- [ ] Do their discoveries match the subjects they enjoy at school?
- [ ] Does their profile match the subjects they find hard at school?
- [ ] Does their profile match the lessons in which they behave negatively? For example, does low linguistic intelligence match poor behaviour in English?

Remind students that we are all good at different things: this is what makes us unique! While some might find Design and Technology easy, for other students this may well be a very difficult lesson because their particular strengths do not lie in this creative area.

Multiple Intelligences – What's It All About?

All of us have heard of IQ – the intelligence quotient.

We hear people talk about how intelligent they are, but there are actually eight different ways to be intelligent, so IQ is only one measure.

You are going to be finding out where your intelligences lie, but first have a look at the list below. A man called Howard Gardner created this list and it is used across the world.

The Eight Different Intelligences

1. **Linguistic**: you like words, poems, crosswords, have good spelling and good vocabulary, and talk through problems.
2. **Logical–mathematical**: you like working with numbers, use lists, are good at logical thinking and enjoy science and maths.
3. **Visual–spatial**: you appreciate the Arts, are good at map reading and jigsaws and enjoy Art.
4. **Bodily–kinaesthetic**: you like sports a lot, think about problems while walking, etc., and like PE.
5. **Musical**: you play an instrument, tap along to music, and whistle and hum.
6. **Interpersonal**: you like working in a group, people come to you for advice and you have quite a few close friends.
7. **Intrapersonal**: you keep a diary or log, like solitary activities, set yourself goals and know yourself well.
8. **Naturalist**: you like animals and biology and are interested in the great outdoors.

This is only a short explanation of each multiple intelligence. Later in this session you will be able to complete a more detailed profile of your intelligences.

On first glance, where do you think your strengths are at the moment?
During your life they will change – some will become more established whereas others will fade into the background.

Famous People – What Kind of Intelligences Do They Have?

Have a look at the following list. What type of intelligence do you think the famous people and others named here have? It could be that they have a mixture of a few. Be ready to explain why you think the way you do.

Refer to the previous handout for help.

	Intelligences
Kylie Minogue	
Alex Ferguson	
Sir David Attenborough	
Your Headteacher	
Lewis Hamilton	
Someone in your family	
Billie Piper	
Johnny Depp	
J. K. Rowling	
Davina McCall	
Sir Alan Sugar	

My Multiple Intelligence Profile

For each section place a number 1 after each statement if you agree that you are 'like' that. Then total up the number 1 scores in each separate section.
Off you go!

Linguistic

You like stories, rhymes and poems. You enjoy wordplay.	
Everything has to be read: books, magazines and comics.	
You feel confident expressing yourself either talking or in writing. You can be a very persuasive debater.	
When you are in conversation you usually talk about things you've read or heard about.	
You like puzzles and crosswords and are a good speller.	
Your vocabulary is brilliant and people comment on it.	
You like English and History at school and enjoy building your vocabulary.	
You can hold your own in a verbal debate or argument and can give clear explanations.	
If you have a problem you tend to 'think out loud', talk through problems and ask questions.	
You take in information easily by listening to CDs, the radio or lectures. The words stay in your mind.	
Total	

Logical–mathematical

You are good at mental calculations and enjoy working with numbers.	
You have an interest in scientific advances and like to 'get inside' the way things really work.	
You are good at managing your money.	
You are the type of person who makes lists and organises an itinerary for any trips.	
You are a good logical thinker when it comes to puzzles and games such as chess or draughts.	
You can easily identify logical flaws in people's conversation.	
You particularly enjoy Maths and Science at school.	
You like programmes about science on the TV.	
You look for patterns and relationships between numbers and take a step-by-step approach to solving problems.	
You like to ask questions about how things work and look for a cause-and-effect chain.	
Total	

Visual–spatial

You have a good colour sense and appreciate the Arts.	
You like to take pictures or video footage to record events.	
You doodle a lot when you are thinking or note taking.	
You are good at reading maps and navigating. Your sense of direction is good.	
You enjoy jigsaws and mazes.	
You are pretty good at taking things apart and putting them back together again. You like kit models.	
You like Art lessons.	
If you need to explain something to someone you will make a diagram or drawing to explain it.	
You can visualise how things might look from a plan.	
If you are reading, you like the book to have plenty of visual illustrations.	
Total	

Bodily–kinaesthetic

You enjoy walking, swimming. In fact, you regularly take part in a sporting activity.	
You are pretty good at DIY – you like having a go!	
You do a lot of your thinking while walking or running.	
If the music is playing, you are up on the dance floor!	
You love the most thrilling rides at the fair.	
You like to handle things – to fiddle with them to fully understand them. You like model making.	
PE is a favourite lesson. You also like lessons where you use your hands – for instance, sculpture.	
If you explain yourself to someone you usually use a lot of hand gestures.	
If you play around with younger children you like to rough and tumble.	
If you are learning something new you like it to be 'hands on' rather than reading from a book or watching a DVD.	
Total	

Musical

You can play a musical instrument.	
If you sing to a song, it's in tune!	
If you hear a tune, you can remember it easily.	
You always have music on at home and like to work listening to it.	
If music is playing, your foot is tapping to it; you have a good sense of rhythm.	
You can hear the different instruments in a band when you listen to music.	
A tune will often just pop into your head.	
You would rather give up the TV than not be able to listen to music.	
You will start to hum or whistle when a tune you like is playing.	
You use rhythm to remember a number or a spelling.	
Total	

Interpersonal

You enjoy working as part of a group.	
You are good at listening to others and helping them to solve their problems.	
Friends will come and talk to you if they need advice.	
You like to take part in team sports.	
You like playing games that involve other people.	
You much prefer being with other people than on your own.	
You have a small group of really close friends.	
You are a good communicator and can help to sort out disputes between other people.	
You like to lead others in an event or task – you like to be in the front!	
If you have a problem, you like to talk it through with a friend rather than dwell on it on your own.	
Total	

Intrapersonal

You like to keep a diary to record your thoughts and feelings.	
You like sitting quietly and reflecting on your life.	
You have goals that you want to achieve and you know what you like and dislike.	
You can make your mind up easily about things.	
You like to do things on your own at times, such as special hobbies, etc.	
You are happy with your own company.	
You tend to prefer a quieter place to noisy places all the time.	
You know what you are good at and what you are not so good at.	
You enjoy learning more about yourself.	
You like just doing your own thing.	
Total	

Naturalist

You really like animals and would like your own pet.	
You can name different birds or plants when you are out and about.	
You like to learn about how the body works.	
If you are outside, you notice things like tracks, birds' nests and wildlife.	
You enjoy activities that take place outdoors.	
You enjoy planting things, watching them grow and tending them.	
You like to know about world environmental issues: you find them interesting.	
You are concerned about the environment and interested in trying to look after the planet.	
You are interested in learning about the human race.	
You like to learn about astronomy (stars).	
Total	

Add up your scores and work out where your natural intelligences lie. Any surprises?

Session 13: Review, Reflection and Progress

This is the final session of the course and is an important time for reflection for each student. This session allows students to re-audit their behaviour and feelings across the curriculum and analyse any changes that have occurred over the period of the course.

It is always useful for this session to prepare and analyse each student's behaviour data before the session. Improvements in behaviour will be clearly seen, with a reduction in negative referral and detentions and fewer fixed period exclusions during the length of the course. This data can then also be used during the session as an indicator to students of the progress they have made.

Secondary SEAL outcomes:

☐ I can communicate effectively with others, listening to what others have to say, as well as expressing my own thoughts and feelings.

☐ I can work well in groups.

☐ I can begin to use my experiences, including mistakes and setbacks, to make appropriate changes to my behaviour.

☐ I can take responsibility for my life, and know how to help myself believe that I can influence what happens to me.

Activity 1: Word Conundrum!

Preparation

- Print/photocopy the 'Word Conundrum' worksheet for each student.
- Print/photocopy the poster 'Success is More About Having the Right Attitude' for each student.

Allow each student 10 minutes to try to unscramble as many as they can of the skills and attitudes they need to stay in school!

A facilitator's answer sheet is included.

Read through each skill and attitude and discuss its importance for the students if they are to stay in school and be successful.

Give each student a copy of the poster about success and attitude to put in their folders. This is a key point so make sure they understand it – having the right attitude is an absolutely essential ingredient in positive behaviour change.

Activity 2: Progress – Lesson Audit

Preparation

☐   Print/photocopy the 'Progress – Lesson Audit' worksheet for each student.

Don't allow students to look back through their folders at their baseline audit from Session 1. Once they have completed the progress audit, analyse each student's progress one by one.

☐   What are the differences?

☐   Why are things different? What has changed?

☐   What have they been doing differently?

☐   Which relationships have improved?

☐   Which subjects have they made the most progress in, and why?

☐   What areas do they need to concentrate on next?

If you have printed off and analysed the students' behaviour data, share it with them.

The Celebration

Preparation

☐   Print out a copy of the 'Certificate of Achievement' for each student; if possible, laminate it.

☐   Invite senior staff and parents to the celebration.

☐   Organise tea, coffee and cakes.

☐   Ask students if they are prepared to give a short talk about their experiences on the Behaviour 4 My Future course.

Award each student a certificate for completing the course. This is a great opportunity to ask key members of staff to attend and show their support, and to give the students praise for the work they have completed during the time they have spent on the course.

Ask those students who have agreed beforehand, to talk about the course and show everyone some of the work from their folders.

It is a time for them to shine!

Success is more about having the right ATTITUDE than how intelligent you are.

Be SMART

Get the right kind of attitude!

Word Conundrum

Have a go at rearranging these words to make a list of skills and attitudes that students need in order to survive in the classroom.

It's a timed task … You have 10 minutes!

☐   O T V A T N M O I I (You have the drive to succeed)

_____

☐   P T C E A C   S B L T I S I Y R E N O I P (You don't blame others)

_____

☐   T E G   H E T   L U L F   C T U P R E I (You stand back and get all the facts first)

_____

☐   F L S E - T R O C O L N (You can stop yourself when you need to)

_____

☐   R E L I E C N E I S (You bounce back when things go wrong)

_____

☐ LFEE OITVPSEI (You need to feel this way!)

_____

☐ KTINH OITPESVI (You need to think this way!)

_____

☐ ARLEN RMOF ITMEKSAS (If you make one of these, you'll need to do this)

_____

☐ MAGEAN ORUY EGSNFEIL (Be in control of these and you'll be OK)

_____

☐ VLUEA LURFOYES (You need to do this for yourself)

_____

☐ TES OALGS (If you have one of these it really helps)

_____

Word Conundrum – Facilitator's Answer Sheet

- ☐ **Motivation**: we know that for the many students who find themselves on the school's Exclusion Stages, without feeling motivated it is unlikely that they will be able to make the changes needed to stay in school. Ask students what affects their motivation.

- ☐ **Accept responsibility**: students who still blame others or make excuses for their poor behaviour are living in a world of external control. We need students to start to accept responsibility and not to say 'yes, but …', 'no, but …'!

- ☐ **Get the full picture**: students need to avoid making decisions to act before they make sure they have all the facts.

- ☐ **Self-control**: a really important part of improving behaviour. Students need to build a repertoire of strategies for avoiding loss of control and the consequences associated with this. These new strategies will need practice if they are to become the automatic responses that students use.

- ☐ **Resilience**: a student who is resilient is someone who doesn't give up when faced with a challenge, bounces back from a disappointment and keeps going even when things get tough.

- ☐ **Feel positive**: many students get bogged down with negative feelings about themselves and their situation at school. These negative feelings affect their behaviour – starting to feel positive is crucial. Ask the students what affects the way they feel. What needs to happen for them to feel more positive?

- ☐ **Think positive**: the way we think affects the way we feel and can also, if we let it, affect our behaviour. Many students just get trapped in a cycle of negative thinking about themselves as individuals and their situation at school. Breaking out of this cycle will be an important part of improving behaviour. Students who think negatively are often students who lack confidence in themselves as learners and have low self-esteem.

- ☐ **Learn from mistakes**: we need to encourage students to think about what it was that went wrong, and how, next time, they could act differently so that their actions will have a more positive outcome.

☐ **Manage your feelings**: students come to school with a whole range of feelings; some are to do with home, while others will be directly related to school – perhaps they are feeling stressed about a particular lesson. Learning to manage this array of feelings is a personal competency that will be beneficial throughout their life, not just at school.

☐ **Value yourself**: understanding themselves, their uniqueness, their strengths and skills will help students to value themselves. Many students whose natural strengths and intelligences lie in skills-based areas, rather than in traditional academic areas, struggle to see their strengths. The introduction of a more skills-based curriculum for Key Stage 4 students allows many of them to begin to feel successful and therefore to value themselves.

☐ **Set goals**: students without a goal often drift along without really putting the 'here and now' together with their future. For many students who make positive changes to their behaviour, it is the identification of a future goal, and the steps they need to take to achieve this, which is the catalyst for change. Ask the students in the group if they have a goal they are striving for.

Progress – Lesson Audit

Name...   Date...

Lesson	Teacher	How much do I enjoy this lesson?	How good is my relationship with this teacher?	Can I do the work in class?	How do I behave in this class?

Certificate of Achievement
for completing the

Behaviour 4
My Future

COURSE

Awarded to

....

Date

....

This student has completed work in the following areas of emotional literacy:

- ☐ Knowing themselves
- ☐ Understanding and managing their feelings
- ☐ Working towards goals
- ☐ Developing their motivation and resilience
- ☐ Evaluating and reviewing their progress
- ☐ Valuing and supporting others
- ☐ Building and maintaining relationships and belonging to a group
- ☐ Solving problems

Awarded by

....

School of Emotional Literacy

The School's mission has always been to create the best chance for every child through the provision of a positive emotional education. From being the first organisation to bring materials for assessing emotional intelligence to Europe, more than 10 years on the School of Emotional Literacy now works in different countries across the world to support and train adults, whether they have a professional or a personal relationship, who work with children. The School firmly believes that by developing children's emotional intelligence, you ensure that they are more likely to be able to reach their potential in the widest sense, helping them to become well-rounded, creative, academically able, happy and socially adept people at the end of their schooling.

The School of Emotional Literacy offers training in a variety of forms to suit individual needs. These include:

- [ ] Accredited Postgraduate Certificate, Diploma and Masters in Emotional Literacy Development.

- [ ] Workshop days related to the practical applications of emotional literacy development, self-esteem building, supporting SEAL, behaviour management and many more.

- [ ] Training the Trainer courses in Peer Support, Restorative Practices and Transforming Relationships.

- [ ] Conferences on all aspects of emotional literacy development.

Above all, the staff at the School of Emotional Literacy are specialised consultants, experts in tailoring their services to suit their individual clients' needs. Being this flexible allows them to offer very effective recommendations to ensure maximum impact and sustainability.

Visit the website www.schoolofemotional-literacy.com for more information.

Also by Susie Davis

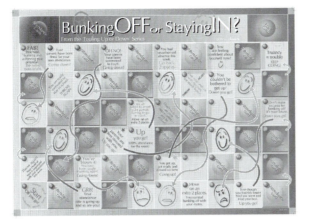

Bunking Off or Staying In?
A unique resource for use with the
thousands of students who every day vote
with their feet and truant from school.

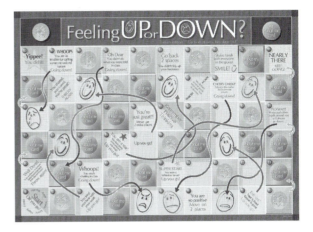

Feeling Up or Down?
Based on the idea of snakes and ladders,
this game helps pupils to learn some of
the key skills and attitudes of emotional
literacy while having fun. Primary and
secondary versions available.

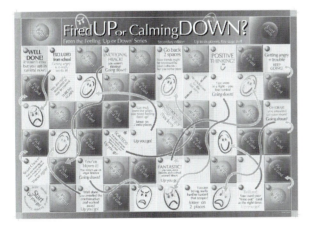

Fired Up or Calming Down?
Following on from *Feeling Up or Down?*,
this version helps children to manage
the feeling of anger successfully.
Primary and secondary versions available.

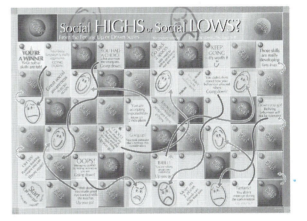

Social Highs or Social Lows?
Children really enjoy the colourful
format of this game as they work through
situations that uncover their perceptions
and choices, and reveal the importance
of sound social skills. Primary and
secondary versions available.

For further information or to place an order contact:
Speechmark Publishing Ltd
70 Alston Drive, Bradwell Abbey, Milton Keynes MK13 9HG, UK

Tel: +44 (0)1908 326944 Fax: +44 (0)1908 326960
Email: sales@speechmark.net Website: www.speechmark.net